Nathaniel Max is a 22 year old transman, from the Lancashire, England. He has found a love of writing, which has helped him to process and survive through all of life's struggles. He lives alone with his rescue cat and is learning to live life on his own terms after years of dysphoria, abuse and mental illness.

For Mazie who taught me to never let anyone dull my rainbow.

And the seventh therapist for helping me find the voice I never knew I had.

Nathaniel Max

ENDURE

AUSTIN MACAULEY PUBLISHERS

LONDON • CAMBRIDGE • NEW YORK • SHARJAH

A CIP catalogue record for this title is available from the British Library.

ISBN 9781035846955 (Paperback)
ISBN 9781035846962 (ePub e-book)

www.austinmacauley.com

First Published 2024
Austin Macauley Publishers Ltd®
1 Canada Square
Canary Wharf
London
E14 5AA

There are so many people who have made such a big impact on my life and although I cannot name them all, they know who they are. I would like to thank Natalie for encouraging me to tell my story, being my biggest cheerleader and my shoulder to cry on. Thank you to my Grandad for his support and always believing in me. Thank you to Ella, Darcey, Nicola and Kirsty for being a part of my story. I want to thank all of the services and support staff that have helped me along the way and the Austin Macauley Publishers for giving me the chance to tell my story.

Table of Contents

Tell Me

How many times do I have to salute a lonely magpie,
Before my sorrow fades?
How many cups of tea do I have to drink,
Before this all feels better?
How many times do I have to go outside,
In good weather,
For the sun to cure my depression?
How loud does my laugh need to be,
Before I actually feel happy?
How many times do I need to go for a walk,
Before my legs want to do it?
How tidy does my home need to be,
For my brain to follow suit?
Tell me what vitamins do you recommend,
To mend my messy mind?
What food will cure my sadness?
And how much water do I need to drink,
Before the bad memories drown?
How many times should I bathe,
To wash my pessimistic attitude away?
And what prayers are most useful,
For a God to ease my pain?
Tell me how to sleep.
I've tried to close my eyes!
Tell me how to breathe.
I've been struggling to do that for a while!
Tell me to talk.
Are you listening to my words?
Tell me how to live.
I wish all these things would work!

The Psych Ward

The psych ward.
That's where I'll be,
Forever haunted by the memories!
The screams,
The silence,
After another life's lost.
Alarms they ring,
Staff run,
The race begins!
Will they save them?
Will they be okay?
You never know,
It goes on,
Night and day.
Scissors are for paper,
But here we use them to cut,
Lines and words,
They bleed,
We're bandaged up.
Blades are for shaving,
But here they are swallowed,
Lost in the winding passages of your gut.
Towels and sheets and clothes,
Anything you can get your hands on,
Tied tightly around your throat.
Nobody asks questions!
The knots are undone,
Or the staff yell for the knife to come!
"Just let me die!"
Your pleas are denied.
Staff would lose their jobs,
If they allowed your dark thoughts to win!
Contraband smuggled in.
"They don't check bras,

Help me get stuff in!"
Patients scale fences,
Slip through open doors,
Running down the road,
A taste of freedom,
The fresh air.
A couple of staff members restrain them,
The chase is over,
A needle to the bum!
Screams echo and bounce off the walls,
They slip under the locked doors,
They keep you awake,
You flinch and feel their pain,
Seclusion is just not humane!
A smiling therapist nods her head,
Saying "That must be hard,"
When you tell her you want to be dead.
And she writes the formulation,
Detailing your traumas in black and white,
Sharing with other professionals,
Even when you shout "No that's not alright!"
Cutlery counted before you leave the room,
Will somebody steal them?
Will they end up in your room?
But the knives are just plastic,
Not worth the effort!
You're still desperate,
But you can wait.
Staff leave boxes of pills on your bed,
The stupid people never check the bags,
They leave you alone instead!
You fight,
You battle,
A war inside your head.
The staff return,
"Oh whoopsies I left these on your bed!"
Hands down their throats,
Vomit in the plant pots,

No, you can't go to the toilet!
You've just eaten,
The rules are rules,
There is no room for bending them!
Confiscated pot noodle lids,
Pebbles from the beach banned,
Toothbrushes checked,
At the matron's demand.
Doors that swing both ways,
Clothing that can't be torn,
Patients that scream,
"I didn't fucking ask to be born!"
New patients shocked,
At the questions asked,
"What you in for then?"
"What was your plan?"
And when phones are taken,
Everybody moans,
Patients shuffle,
Wrapped up tightly in blankets,
Playing card games,
Until somebody throws the table.
Fists pound against the punch bag,
It's the lad that cries himself to sleep,
Swearing and sweating.
And there's that one girl that screams,
"It's not fucking fair,
I just want to go home!"
There's a birthday cake,
In the kitchen,
For the patient,
That's been here too long.
Her family don't visit anymore,
This ward has become her home.
And you sit under the desk,
Hands clamped to your ears,
Staff notice you're missing,
But you don't want to be found!

And then a girl sees your feet,
Whispers "make some room for me!"
And you put your head on her shoulder,
As you both fall asleep.
Patients become friends,
Memories made together,
A love that will never end,
You've seen the worst together,
This friendship will surely last forever?
You've seen their scars,
Their fresh self-harm,
Held them whilst they cried,
Watched them almost die,
You scream for help,
but staff are too busy chatting for you to be heard,
So you restrain your friend yourself,
Undo the knots from their neck,
Or wrestle a blade from their grasp,
You will never give up on them,
Not even when they beg,
Just let me go!
The medications are thrown at you,
Doses upped.
It still isn't working!
Maybe a different pill?
This one makes you a zombie,
But still!
The straighteners left in your room,
Idiot staff members,
They just assume!
They thought you could handle it,
They thought wrong!
They come back and take them from your skin.
Your mum asks "How are you?"
Oh no, where the fuck do I begin?
You sit and you stare,
The white walls,
The chemicals in the air,

It's too clinical here!
You feel like you've been here for years!
Nobody helps you,
You're expected just to get better,
Like magic.
They'll take the credit,
And wave goodbye before you're ready,
You'll be back soon,
They know it and so do you!
But for now, you're free,
And you've got nothing to lose!
You look back sometimes,
You shudder at the past,
But Mazie she lived there,
It was where you saw her last!
The staff never understood,
They never helped at all.
But some of them were kind,
Just had no chance to help at all.
The last place you want to be,
Is in the walls of A&E,
Waiting to be admitted to a place where this is what your life
will be.

Do You Know Me At All?

If you only think of me as sweet,
With words that stay polite,
You haven't felt the bitterness I hold,
How my mind can't let go,
Of the things I've seen.
If you imagine me always standing,
You haven't seen the days,
When all I can do is crawl,
Forcing my body to move,
So you never see me stop at all.
If you think I only ever smile,
Look a little closer,
And you might notice,
It doesn't quite reach my eyes.
If you think I'm invincible,
Did you ever watch me fall,
Over and over and over again,
Or did you just see me get back up?
If you haven't seen me cry,
Think that I never shed a tear,
Do you know my story at all?
Have you heard my biggest fears?
If you think I am cold,
You mustn't understand how I love at all,
That I give and give and give,
Until I lose it all.
If you think I don't make time for you,
You haven't seen my diary fill up,
My days are filled with other people's plans,
And I cannot split myself in half,
To be in two places at once.
If you think I am composed,
You haven't noticed the moments that I turn away,
Hiding the shaking of my hands,

Or the change in my face.
If you think that I never talk about the hard stuff,
Were you there when hard things were all I knew?
If you think I am embarrassed by the details,
Have you tried to talk at all,
Or did you just assume?
If you think I am crazy,
What would a sane response be?
How would a sane person react,
If they experienced,
All of the things that almost killed me?
If you think my lips don't know,
How to say the words you're thinking,
Then you haven't heard my rants,
Where all the swear words and truths,
Come flowing out of my mouth.
If you think I always understand,
It's because I'm hurting too,
And I'll be damned if another person,
Feels this alone when I'm in the room.
So when you see a smiling person,
Who never seems to stop,
Always seems to understand,
Remember they are human too.
They might fall apart a thousand times,
And then put themselves back together,
In time for the sunrise.
They might spend a few moments,
Practicing their fake smile in the mirror,
Telling themselves that they are okay,
Despite their face still burning from last night's tears.
They might always understand,
Always say the right words,
Because they have written a script in their minds,
Titled "*Things I wish I could hear*".
So look a little closer,
Ask a few more questions,

And stop assuming that people are okay,
Just because you see your smile mirrored.

Just Breathe

Inhale,
Exhale.
Inhale,
Exhale.
Just breathe!
I have to remind myself,
How to do that.
I have to remind myself,
To allow my lungs,
To consume the oxygen,
As though it is a choice,
As though breathing is an option.
I have to remind myself to breathe,
Because something that,
Should be instinctive,
Has been cancelled,
By the need to stay silent,
To go unnoticed and unheard.
You taught me,
That the one thing,
That keeps me alive,
Could be the thing that,
Puts me in danger!
And now whenever I am scared,
My lungs freeze,
My mouth seals shut,
And I shrink further into myself,
Holding myself in the foetal position,
Protecting my head.
You taught me to fear living,
And it is that fear,
That takes up residence,
In my body,
Every night.

It's 3 am,
And I know that,
Because of the colour of the sky,
My racing mind,
And my pounding heart.
My eyes fix themselves on the door,
And I cannot breathe,
I cannot move,
I am trapped,
Between what was and what is.
It is a place,
Where the traumatised version of me lives!
That small kid version of me,
Who still waits for you,
To appear at the door.
I am already gripping the sheets,
And waiting for the inevitable.
I am prepared to protect,
My little sister at all costs!
I am ready to face the shadow man,
Like I do every fucking night!
But he is late,
And I can't move.
Because getting out of bed,
Is what naughty children do!
And so I lie there,
And wait.
And wait.
Hoping it will be over soon,
But when I look around the room,
I realise I am being silly!
My sister is carrying her own baby,
I am alone,
And the cat sat on the end of the bed,
Isn't a stranger's!
She is mine,
And I am home.

A Letter to Self-Harm

You have been around more than my family,
You stuck by me when my friends didn't!
You slipped into my life,
Promised to be my friend,
But you wanted to stay a secret,
That way nobody could keep us apart.
But your friendship was a toxic disguise!
You groomed me from the very start,
To believe you'd be the one thing,
To help me.
Now I realise:
You told me you could solve every problem,
But you failed to mention,
That you'd only create more!
You dictated what I wore,
Told me my sleeves had to be long,
Made me hide my thighs,
To avoid everybody's eyes.
And before I knew it,
There was no part of me I could show!
Even my face had to be hidden,
Behind plasters and gauze,
After you left me sore.
Showers always stung,
Like needles from head to toe,
You stained the walls,
Turned my baths pink,
And when I tried to leave you,
You whispered:
"But I can help you forget the past,
I'll make the present easier to bear,
And I'll be the one to keep you alive,
With me by your side, a future is there!"
So I take your hand once more.

A blade stuck to the sink,
Scissors by my bedside,
Stockpiled pills in hidden bags,
And torn clothing.
"You feel better right?"
But I don't feel better anymore!
My skin feels rather sore,
I've got a bald patch on my head.
I've needed X-rays,
Medication,
Antibiotic prescriptions.
I've run out of dressings,
And bandages too,
I needed surgery to rectify the damage,
You made me do!
I've been sent away from home,
Multiple times,
To detach myself from you out of sight.
See nobody wants to be around me anymore.
All they see are cuts and blisters,
Bruises and scars,
And they are scared that saying the wrong things,
Will make me run back into your arms!
I check everyone's wrists,
For scars like mine.
And when I see somebody cry,
I am automatically scared,
That they have fallen for you,
Because so did I.
Now I see nothing the same,
Everything has a use!
And I always seem to run back to you,
Because you always seem to understand,
You help me forget.
And when I am in physical pain,
I am at least not feeling anything else,
It's just you and me instead.
But you are no friend!

You forced me to lie:
Say, I'm okay,
A billion times.
And the cuts only get deeper!
The burns more frequent,
The ligatures become tighter,
And the hospital rooms get quieter.
Because nobody knows what to say,
When you hurt yourself every day.
But friends aren't supposed to cause you pain!

My Four-Legged Purpose

I used to stay in bed.
The weight was too heavy,
I couldn't move.
So I'd pull the duvet up,
Lie there feeling low,
And wouldn't even eat or drink,
I had just given up.
But now in the mornings,
I drag myself out of bed,
Because I know your little face will be waiting,
You need comforting through the day ahead.
And seeing you run towards me,
Meowing so loud,
Like you have craved my attention all night,
And you can't quite believe your luck,
And seeing how happy you are to see me,
Reminds me that I am loved.
I can't wallow in self-pity,
I can't let my feelings consume me,
I can't give up,
I can't end it,
Because you need me!
And though I tell myself,
You'd be better off with somebody else,
I know it isn't true,
That is just a lie I tell myself,
So I'll do it for you.
On the good days,
And on the bad,
Because you deserve better,
Than wondering,
Why I never came back.

The Seventh Therapist

The seventh therapist listens,
I can see it in her eyes.
She talks to me like I'm human,
Not just an illness,
She isn't looking at the time.
The seventh therapist listens,
She isn't judging me at all!
She hears my story,
Without running,
And encourages me to talk.
The seventh therapist listens,
She is happy to sit on the floor,
She doesn't take notes in front of me,
Or constantly watch the door.
The seventh therapist listens,
With tears in her eyes.
She hears every little detail,
The change in my voice,
And all of the things I hate about myself,
She doesn't despise.
The seventh therapist listens,
I've seen so many before!
They all come with their own methods,
Try to dive into my brain,
But most of them don't really listen,
It makes me feel insane.
But this therapist is different!
She sits with me in my pain,
Holds my head when I'm seizing,
And tells me it's going to be okay.
The seventh therapist listens,
She reads between the lines,
Offers words of comfort,
And swears from time to time.

The seventh therapist listens,
She catches each "I don't know",
In her hands,
Sticks by me for three years,
Just to give me a chance.
She doesn't let me give up on myself,
She lets me cry,
And each time I say I've had enough,
She listens to all of the reasons why.
The seventh therapist listens,
As I tell my story for the first time.
Discarding the tape,
Stuck to my mouth,
That's been keeping me silent,
For a while.
The seventh therapist listens,
She tries her best to understand.
And in doing so,
She hands me the strength,
I haven't felt in a long time,
So it finally feels like there is a future,
I can call mine.
The seventh therapist listens,
Without her, I wouldn't be alive!
Taking the time to get to know me,
She sits by my side,
And each time I get stuck in the dark,
She shows me a sunrise.
The seventh therapist listens,
We've since said goodbye.
Her parting gifts,
In the shape of:
Hope,
Strength,
Validation,
And the confidence to live my own life!
The seventh therapist listens,
I promise you she does!

So if you're losing hope,
Sick of being told it's your fault,
When nobody sees where you started,
Hold on because:
The seventh therapist listens.

Transgender

This Is the Real Me

I am trans.
It doesn't make sense to you,
You don't quite understand.
When you use the wrong pronouns,
Call me by my old name,
Treat me differently,
A part of me dies on the inside,
And I'm reminded,
That I will never truly be seen,
As the real me.
I've fought through years,
Of pretending to be somebody I'm not,
Just to make you happy,
To blend in,
To not make things *complicated*.
But being trans is not a choice!
The only thing I chose,
Was to use my voice!
To speak up,
And say,
This is who I am!
And your validation,
Isn't something I need!
But it would help me,
As I become the real me,
To see that you aren't ashamed,
Of the person I am,
Because this is who I have been all along!
And the dresses,

And makeup,
And long hair,
Were just an uncomfortable disguise,
Until I was ready,
To be who I was always meant to be.
And I know sometimes,
It makes you feel unsure,
So when you see me starting to change,
My hair,
My clothes,
You feel like you're losing,
The person you loved.
But I am still the same person,
On the inside!
And although my body,
Will not stay the same,
It will be different over time,
Who I am will not.
You loved my disguise,
The question is,
Can you accept,
The person beneath?
Because after all,
This is the real me.

Body parts

Why is it that body parts,
Equal,
A label of Woman or Man?
Like having boobs,
Is all it means to be a woman?
But what about the breast cancer patients,
Who's double mastectomies saved their lives?
Do their flat chests make them,
Any different on the inside?
And why does the ability to carry a child,
Make you female?
When there are so many women,
Out there that can't!
They spend their lives,
Having miscarriages,
Trying IVF and surgeries and injections,
Until their hope runs out.
Then there's the women who become menopausal,
After years of periods and cramps.
Who brought life into the world,
Raised families,
And now have reached an age,
Where their bodies relieve them,
Of the menstruation pains.
They are still strong women!
That never changes,
Despite their inability to conceive,
Who they are inside remains the same!
So why should owning a vulva,
Make a difference?
When all it means,
Is sitting down to pee?
And why does having a vagina matter,
When it affects nobody but me?

And what about the young men,
That never quite grow facial hair?
Their face still bare like babies,
Yet they can still drink and swear!
What about the men with testicular cancer,
That undergo surgeries to remove the lumps?
But they are still the same men they were before,
Just a bit more scarred and sore.
What about the men who went off to war,
Got blown to bits and bodies deformed?
Yet they still remained men!
Despite their missing limbs,
They were no different than before.
All of these people have their labels,
Not defined by genitals at all!
Just a word to describe,
Who they feel they are on the inside.
So why,
When I say I am a man,
When I force my chest into binders,
Pack my underwear with prosthetics,
Cut my hair shorter,
Try to dress what is deemed masculine.
Do people still spew excuses of:
"But it's so hard!"
"It's confusing!"
And why do they still use the word woman?
Still call me a she?
When I am practically screaming:
Just let me be me!

Dysphoria

Gender isn't binary,
You can be who you want to be!
Then why is it that so many people,
Have an issue with me,
Being me?
They have a million questions!
A clipboard that will confirm,
Or deny my identity.
Being born into a body that doesn't fit:
It doesn't fit who I am,
It doesn't fit my soul,
It is too small,
I keep wishing I'd grow!
It feels soul-crushing!
And when a cis person asks,
Questions like:
So what's in your pants now?
Will you get your boobs off?
Will your clit really grow?
Won't your beard look patchy?
Do you want a dick,
Or is a strap-on easier?
I feel myself start to float.
I try to educate,
I agree to let them take notes,
But my life is not,
A case study,
You can't decide how this story goes!
If the scalpel slices my skin,
And the breast tissue is discarded,
As nothing more than medical waste,
If the sutures are done neatly,
And scars are all that remain.
If my chest is flattened,

And there's a smile on my face,
Then why does it fucking matter?
It's my choice to make!
And you can keep your unsolicited advice,
Lock it up tight within a box,
Drop it off a cliff's edge.
Bring your damaging opinions,
To a stop.
I can do whatever the fuck I want!
If I decide to inject myself,
To let the hormones flow in my veins,
To be medicated for,
The remainder of my life,
Then I have a mind that can't be changed!
If my voice begins to deepen,
And facial hair makes an appearance,
If my muscles grow easier,
Then my smile will grow too!
Nobody wants to go through,
A second puberty!
But I feel like I've been living a lie,
And it is getting more dangerous,
To force myself to hide.
You don't understand how hard it is,
To not just end my life,
Or take the blade to my own body,
To make things look right.
And if I decide to go,
Under the knife,
To change the way my genitals appear.
So that the shame can leave me,
And the phantom limb syndrome,
Can finally disappear.
Then that's my choice to make!
And if you're so concerned,
With what's between my legs,
Maybe that's your problem,
To work on,

Stop judging me instead.
Because this gender dysphoria,
Is a killer!
It has taken more lives,
Than you have heard of!
And being transgender isn't a choice,
The doctor made a mistake,
When he disclosed,
The gender assigned to me at birth,
Before I was five minutes old!
And I have been fighting ever since,
To tell the world,
That isn't who I am!
This body isn't mine!
But I can transition,
Into the person,
I have always been.
And one day,
Maybe I will finally feel seen.

They Don't Hate Me
for My Gender

They say the doctors and nurses,
View your body as another problem to diagnose,
That they've seen it all before,
They don't sexualise,
Or judge,
What lies beneath your clothes.
But I felt her eyes stare at my chest,
Zoning in on the parts of me,
I hate the most.
I want the ground to swallow me up,
When she asks,
'So are you going through the change then?'
And I try to act confident,
To be unbothered,
But then she whisks me away,
To another place,
And the nurses begin to whisper.
They look,
They laugh,
I am their clown,
The hospital my circus,
Like they are waiting for my next trick,
Scared of my body changing,
Morphing,
When they blink.
And I blame it on the professional,
Lifting up my shirt,
With those judging eyes,
Seeing boobs,
Instead of a flat chest.
And she forgot about my heart,
The reason I neededs help,

I wonder if she saw my pulse spike?
Watched it break,
As I realised,
I will never be accepted,
In this kind of place.
I am seen as something inhuman,
A caged tiger in a zoo,
Stared at,
Mocked,
But feared all the same.
People don't hate me for my gender,
They hate the way they feel afraid.
The threat I pose is minimal,
But they don't want to accept change!
They would rather separate us into boxes,
Defined by sex organs given at birth,
I show them all the things that,
They lack within.
The sureness of who I am,
My ability to embrace change,
To talk about my body with honesty,
To bare my flaws,
Blue and pink and white,
Instead of hiding away in the dark,
I stand firmly in the light.
They are scared of the lengths I'd go to,
To look at how I feel on the inside,
When they are happy in their comfort,
Where nothing changes,
Challenges,
Or puts up a fight.
But these professionals have powers,
That they don't even see,
They can show the world that bodies,
Are not all what they seem.
And sometimes even doctors,
And nurses,
Have flaws and insecurities.

But with kindness, they can change lives,
A reassuring smile,
Communication techniques,
A closed curtain or cover sheet.
A hand to hold,
Ears to listen,
And tongue to speak up for people like me.
To remind everybody that,
Trans rights are human rights!
And they aren't that much different from me.

Trans Joy

A binder lets me hold you.
It compresses my chest enough,
That I forget the unwanted breasts,
Even sit there!
My cheeks ache from smiling,
My new T-shirts finally getting worn,
And my back is no longer hunched.
It's freedom!
A validating hug,
Invisible to most.
Eight hours of flat-chested happiness,
Of breathing easier,
Of moving my body without worrying.
This is trans joy!
Euphoria!
Every second making the last twenty years,
Feel like a lifetime ago.
The NHS waiting lists are long,
But I have a newly found hope,
That my future,
Will be beautiful.
That everyday will be flat-chested,
That I will stand topless on the beach,
With only two small lines,
Reminding me of what once was.
That one day,
The mirror will be my assistant,
As I attempt to shave my face,
No longer the beard of my dreams,
But one I can touch and shape!
That one day,
My voice will be low in pitch,
I won't have to correct people on the phone,
They will hear the masculine energy,

And not question it at all.
That one day,
I will stand before a mirror,
Feeling totally complete,
No need to worry about bleeding,
I'll be able to stand to pee!
All of these hopes come from this binder,
If this can give me a glimpse,
At happiness,
Then with medications and surgeries,
I might finally be free!

Loss

I Am Good At Losing Things

I am good at losing things!
Coats and jumpers,
Socks and ties,
Even my phone.
My mum would say I'd lose my head,
If it wasn't screwed on.
And I wonder if she knew that eventually,
I would unravel?
The books throwing themselves,
From the shelves,
Of the library in my mind,
Pages of memories flying,
At me from seemingly nowhere,
Leaving me a confused wreck.
I lost my mind,
I am good at losing things!
I wonder if she knew,
That I would say more goodbyes,
Than I could handle.
That I would refine the technique,
Learn to smile and wave,
As though everything was okay,
And then as soon as they left,
I was free to break!
Shattering,
Collapsing in on myself,
And then forcing each broken piece,
Back into its place.
Finding a new oddly shaped hole,
Where they used to be.

My life,
Forever changed.
I am good at losing things.
And I am tired of my unintentional talent,
It is not one I am proud of,
It is not one that makes me smile.
It is a heartbreaking reality,
That loving people,
Comes at a cost!
And I paid with my fractured mind,
And a broken heart.
I am good at losing things.

23/06/2018

June 23rd 2018,
The day you left,
10 pm,
You were found,
In the woods.
No goodbyes,
Just a dozen warning signs!
I begged them to hear me!
I begged them to save you!
I tried so hard,
To make them see,
You weren't as okay,
As they believed.
I held you so many times,
Saw the tears on your face,
Heard your words,
Saw the way your smile faltered,
The way your eyes glazed over,
When you thought nobody was watching.
The way you'd come and wake me up,
Throwing tiny packs of butter at my head,
Most mornings to demand your breakfast.
Red rings would mark your neck,
All of those nights you'd tried to leave,
They accused you of trying to attention seek!
But I heard your panicked cries,
Saw your hands shake,
Watched you hyperventilate.
And you'd grip my hand,
And scream and yell,
And I used to wish it was me,
Going through your kind of hell.
And you'd whisper to me,
"I hate them. I just want it to stop"

I'd tell you I understood.
And you were safe now,
That it was fucked up,
That it wasn't okay!
And I'd promise I would stay by your side,
Visit you all the time,
That if either of us died,
We'd haunt each other,
If there was such a thing,
As an afterlife!
You looked me in the eyes,
"Would you adopt me if you could?"
Without missing a beat I nodded my head,
Said "Of course, I would! You're a good kid!"
And I watched your face light up,
As you called me your shit cove mum,
And I gave you a hug,
Told you it was going to be okay,
That you were loved.
And I thought that things might get better,
You shared your story with me,
One dark memory at a time,
And I told you bits of mine.
We told each other things,
We'd never dare say out loud,
To anybody else.
In fact-
You never did!
You left us before you had that chance.
The day you left,
You took a piece of me with you,
Left a Mazie-shaped hole in my life.
Made it feel impossible,
For me to stay alive,
Without my crazy best friend by my side.
You were just a kid!
You had more dreams than I ever did.
Full of life,

Full of love,
And now the rooms don't light up.
Your songs remain unwritten,
The guitar is left gathering dust,
The stage you could have been on,
Stays empty,
And the audience will never hear your voice.
Because you didn't just leave your past behind,
You left a beautiful future too!
And since the day I heard of your death,
And read the eulogy I wrote,
The one that annoyed me so much,
Because no matter how hard I tried,
Words just couldn't sum you up!
I've felt empty too.
But though it hurts like hell,
And life just isn't the same,
I respect your decision,
Despite my own pain.
This world did you wrong,
You deserved so much love,
And I hope you're at peace now,
No longer tormented,
And you knew,
You were loved,
The day you chose to leave this world behind.
Because your memory will forever live on,
In my mind!
And I'll share your story slowly,
So one day everybody will know,
Of the girl who was bubbly,
And kind,
And was bent to an extent,
And made everybody smile!

And who's dream it was to sing on stage with her guitar,
Who sang like an angel,
Until the day she became one.
The girl who showed me,
What it truly means to be alive.

Grief

Grief has me in its clutches.
Sometimes it's a demon,
That follows me wherever I go.
It shows me:
Where I went wrong,
What I could have done to save you,
It tells me that it's all my fault.
That it should have been me,
Not you!
Grief has me in its clutches,
Sometimes it's a child.
Wanting to be held,
As it cries in pain,
With an innocent confusion,
That never seems to fade.
Constantly prodding,
And poking me,
Turning my head,
Saying:
"Look! Remember that?"
Then I see something that reminds me of you.
Grief has me in its clutches.
Sometimes it's like a vacuum,
That sucks me up,
Like I am nothing but a few crumbs,
Scattered on the floor.
It sends me spinning into a pile of "What ifs",
And I'm lost trying to find my way out,
And pull myself back together,
Into something that resembles,
Something relatively whole.
Grief has me in its clutches.
Sometimes it's a never-ending pit,
Or rabbit hole,

And I am Alice,
Falling,
Down,
Down,
Down.
Watching the memories,
Both good and bad,
Flash before my eyes:
Your smile,
Your laugh,
Your tears,
Your pain.
And just when I hit the bottom,
I'm falling yet again!
Grief has me in its clutches,
Sometimes it's a teenager.
Stomping around,
Slamming doors,
Screaming at the unfairness of it all!
It swears,
It rants,
It blames the world,
For the unbearable reality,
That you are really gone!
Grief has me in its clutches.
Sometimes it's an old lady,
Sat rocking in a chair,
Reminiscing of the past,
While nobody listens,
They don't care!
They don't want to hear stories,
Of somebody, they never knew,
And the old lady is just seen as daft,
Stuck in the past.
But she keeps rocking in her chair,
Knitting repetitive stitches,
And if you look closely,
You'll see,

The wool has formed the words,
"I'm so sorry,
I hope you know I cared"
Grief has me in its clutches,
Sometimes it's a new puppy.
Bounding along,
Looking at the world with fresh eyes,
Tasting everything in sight,
Wanting to be friends with everyone,
Wanting everyone to be alright.
Playing games,
Chasing everything around,
Desperate to see the world,
Desperate to be heard.
Almost like that puppy's whines,
Are saying:
"I'll make the most of my life for you"
Grief has me in its clutches,
Sometimes it's a jigsaw.
So many pieces,
Different shapes and sizes,
Each piece a memory.
A person,
A place.
But when I tip the box upside down,
Check the floor too,
There's one piece always missing,
And that piece is always you.
Grief has me in its clutches,
Sometimes it's like the sea.
The waves rise,
And fall,
And crash,
On the shore.
But if you look further out,
You will see:
There's an ocean that is deeper,
And darker,

And more dangerous.
Full of memories,
To drown in,
If I stay here,
Wearing your old jumper,
With your photographs,
At my feet.
Grief has me in its clutches,
Sometimes it's a song.
That plays until the part,
Where a chorus should be.
But instead,
The verses continue,
And the song,
Doesn't quite flow.
It has no meaning,
No relevance,
No story,
And I'm left wondering,
What it would have sounded like.
Grief has me in its clutches.
And it will never let go.
It's a never-ending feeling,
Of wondering why on earth you had to go!
And my questions will go unanswered,
Your story will stay as it was.
A sentence stopped,
Right in the middle,
And I didn't get to hear,
The rest of it,
Or what your very last line was.

Platonically, Obviously!

Platonic.
The first time I heard that word,
Was in a ward,
Where relationships were scrutinised.
Yellow letters pressed into hands,
And the word love,
Was followed by raised eyebrows,
Of the nurses' disapproval.
I remember the goofy smiles that dropped.
The teenagers dressed in scars,
Like patchwork dolls made of dressings,
Rolling their eyes,
"I meant platonically, obviously!"
The need to say:
Not like that,
Just as friends!
Like sisters,
Like sponsors!
Spewing from her lips.
And back then I laughed,
Rolled my eyes too,
Waited for the nurse to leave,
Before I whispered,
"I love you too, dummy"
And now I wish I had screamed it!
That I'd pulled you into my arms,
That I'd told you over and over,
To "please hold on"
I didn't realise those three words,
Meant more than you let on.
It meant goodbye.
It meant I need you to know I care!
It meant this meant something more,
Than just being patients in the same ward.

We'd put all of our problems into one big pile,
And halved them,
Shared some crazy memories along the way.
We used sign language most of the time,
Our two middle fingers,
Pressed into our palm,
Shaking our hands side to side,
No words,
Able to be criticised.
And I didn't realise I'd miss those fleeting moments,
Or be so angry at that nurse,
I could scream!
Because they made it something that it wasn't,
Painted us in shame,
For simply reminding each other:
You're loved,
You matter,
Please stay.

A Nod To You

It is the little things,
That bring you closer.
Like Lynx Africa,
Animals you'd have fawned over.
And there you are again,
Standing there in full colour.
Ben & Jerry's cookie dough,
A coke,
And dominoes,
All of those things make me wonder,
Why you had to go?
Because I can still hear your laughter,
As you threw chips at my face.
And I still find myself,
Listening to your favourite songs,
Wishing more than anything,
That I could hear you sing along.
I used to spend every day with you,
By my side!
And now you are everywhere,
On cold starry nights,
With only myself to wrap,
In fluffy blankets.
In the warm sunshine,
With only one spoon needed,
To eat ice cream with.
In the bad weather,
With a rainbow in the sky,
But without you there to smile at it.
And anytime I begin to cry,
I remember it isn't what you'd want!
So I fill my days with colour,
And sunshine,
And laughter,

And all of the foods,
You used to beg me to eat.
And with each moment,
That I chose to stay,
It is a nod to your memory,
And the girl who begged me to live.

Trauma

That 1% Isn't Enough

I want to ask why.
Why do you peck at me,
Prod me,
Poke me,
Mock me?
Why do you leave me,
When I'm of no use to you?
And then just as I decide,
I'm leaving too,
You turn back around,
Say all of the right things,
Give me a hug,
And offer words of love.
It is only moments later,
That the old routine begins!
You push me,
Throw your cruel words at me,
And make me feel like,
I am no bigger than a pea!
I tell myself you'll change,
That you were nice to me just yesterday,
That this is just one of your bad days.
But this is the version of you,
That I see 99% of the time,
The 1% I love,
Is not enough to hold on to!
So all I want to know now is,
Why do you occasionally act like you care,
Only to use me as a verbal punching bag,
How is it fair?

Am I the Narcissist?

Am I the narcissist?
I ask myself late at night,
As though if I was the problem,
It would make it all alright.
I have been the common denominator,
In every abusive situation,
With family,
And fucked up exes,
It was always me,
That they screamed at!
It was always me,
That they let their fists swing into!
It was always my fault,
They'd tell me that,
Over and over and over again,
"Get it into your thick skull".
So I'd tell them I was sorry,
And we'd all move on.
But the apologies weren't sincere,
Because how can you mean it,
When you don't know,
What you've done wrong?
So I started telling myself,
There's just something wrong with me!
I need to do better!
I need to be good!
And when that didn't quite work:
I need to listen more!
I need to stop talking!
And when I finally realised,
That all of my energy was being drained,
By people who handed me all of the blame,
And hope was running out,
My desperation rising.

I started to try to leave,
In any way I could.
Because I was the problem, right?
So take me out of the equation,
And at least their lives would be good!
But no matter how hard I tried,
I couldn't end my stupid little life.
And so things continued to spiral,
I didn't know what to do.
Because what do you do,
When the people you love the most,
Don't love you too?
So I did what I do best,
When things get hard,
And I ran away,
Started a new life,
Away from my family,
Thinking I'd be safe.
But these thoughts and feelings,
Are rooted in my brain.
I don't know what to do!
I don't know what to say!
All I've ever known,
Is this fucking pain!
So what do you do,
When you feel like you're going insane?
You search for an answer,
To heal your broken brain.
And so I start asking myself:
Am I the narcissist?
Am I the problem?
Am I the rotten orange,
That needs to be discarded?
Because I am so tired of this pain,
Of everyone pointing their finger,
In my direction,
Each time something goes wrong,
I'm the one they blame!

All I want is everyone to be okay.
I'm not sure I can trust myself,
I'm not sure if I can trust this brain.
See the thing is,
I'm chained to them by DNA and a last name,
And I never know what's right!
You see loving is so much harder,
When you've felt like this your whole life.
So I am careful of who I trust,
Scared of falling for another mask.
Because their smiles are disguises,
A fake persona for the rest of the world,
Because nobody wants to be seen,
Not for the monster they are!
So it stays behind closed doors,
Where nobody goes.
You lie,
You pretend,
You follow the rules,
And *oh there's so many rules!*
So you stay locked away,
In their cruel embrace,
Maybe it will get better one day?
Maybe it will all go away?
I can fix them I know it!
If I just love them enough,
They'll change!
But you lose more of yourself every day.
So choose carefully,
Because monsters wear disguises,
And you could scream,
You could yell,
But they would only drag you deeper,
Into the pits of hell.

Redecorating

I grew up in a world stripped of love.
No kind compliments.
No soothing hugs,
When I cried,
No hand to hold,
When things didn't feel alright.
There was no smiling face,
To tell me it was all okay.
There was nobody telling me,
To reach for the stars,
That I could do,
Anything I set my mind to,
Or work towards what I want.
Instead, I was handed harsh realities,
Coached into accepting rough hands,
And trained to be grateful,
For the fleeting moments of affection.
The words "I love you",
Were just what people said,
Not some heartfelt reminder or vow.
And I listened to threats,
And nasty names,
Took them on the chin,
Like it was a cute nickname,
And not the most insulting words to say!
I grew up in a world stripped of love.
But I've been painting my world,
In brand new colours!
And I show people I care,
With all of the reassuring smiles,
I was never given!
All of the hugs,
That I didn't receive!
And all of the words,

I needed to hear back then!
And I am everyone's personal cheerleader.
Telling them that they can do,
Absolutely anything they want.
I make sure my hands are always kind,
So nobody flinches at them moving,
Or follows them with their eyes!
I make sure people feel seen and heard.
I haven't been shown how to love,
But I have been taught,
What is hurtful.
So I make it my mission,
To give compliments freely,
To only say "I love you",
When I really mean it!
To make big gestures of appreciation,
Even if they make me look daft,
The smile on their faces,
Makes it all worth it!
And to make sure everybody knows,
My arms will always be a safe place,
For them to run to,
And my shoulder is free to cry on.
I grew up in a world stripped of love!
But I am redecorating,
So nobody else knows,
How it feels,
To never feel good enough.

If Walls Could Talk

If only the walls could testify.
If only they could sit in a video interview,
Spew the details of his actions,
So I wouldn't have to!
Those walls saw it all,
My only witnesses,
Mouths plastered shut.
If only the walls could testify:
Maybe then my words would be believed?
Maybe the walls could talk more in-depth,
More descriptive,
More bluntly,
Than I could at sixteen.
If only the walls could testify:
Maybe you wouldn't have continued,
To hurt me.
They could have screamed,
When I couldn't!
If only the walls could testify:
Maybe you would be behind bars?
Rotting in a cell somewhere,
Instead of holding my nephew in your arms!
Maybe seeing you be convicted,
Would give me some peace?
Maybe it would save your future victims,
Maybe it would have saved me!
If only the walls could testify:
They could have soothed me.
Whispered reassurances,
As I stared at the ceiling,
Showed me a secret exit,
To flee.
If only the walls could testify:
Maybe I wouldn't live in fear?

Maybe I wouldn't be so quiet?
I would be able to speak,
To tell the world my story,
Without a lawsuit finding me!
If only the walls could testify:
Maybe I wouldn't feel so alone?
Maybe I would be able to talk to them,
Find validation in corroboration.
If only the walls could testify:
Maybe I could move on?
It's funny how your life's the same,
Mine changed forever,
When I realised,
Walls cannot talk!
And nobody else would ever come forward,
To confirm the truth,
So it's always going to be,
Me against You.

The Wild Card

You say I was the wild card,
The unexpected surprise.
I feel myself recoil.
You say it like the bad taste in your mouth.
You say it with a longing,
For who you thought I was.
You say it with a bitterness,
As though I am a lemon,
You have just bitten into.
And I stand back,
As though I have been slapped.
All my life has been:
Serving you,
Sticking to your rules,
Pleasing you.
Folding myself,
Smaller and smaller,
Until I was the child,
Who was seen and not heard.
The child you could glimpse,
From the corner of your eye,
But when you turned to look,
It was as though I hadn't been there at all,
And that was how you liked it.
You had taught your daughter well,
She would dry your tears,
You could collapse into her arms,
And her sweet little smile,
Would never waver.
She would be everything you needed,
Like a walking safe you could store,
All of your secrets in,
Knowing that only you,
Could break the combination.

And now when you see me:
I do not hide,
I do not run,
I enunciate every word,
And my smile is for me alone.
I was never your daughter!
I am your son.
You want to rewind the clock,
To fold me back,
Into your neat little box,
And tie me down,
With a pretty pink bow on top?
But I am my own person,
With my own thoughts and feelings,
And I answer to no one!
I am not your parent,
I am your son.

The Fist

I keep racking my brain,
Searching for the moment in time,
When you changed.
But the more I sift through memories,
The more I realise,
What was right in front of my face.
The truth was you never changed,
You have always been the same!
When I have to describe you,
To people who haven't heard your name,
I say you that were my father,
Instead of the voice,
Criticising me,
From the back of my brain.
I remember you in flashes:
A bald man,
Livid eyes darkening,
Eyebrows drawn together,
Mouth spitting and slurring insults at me.
I remember you:
As the staggering,
Stumbling,
Alcohol fuelled nightmare,
Who swung his clenched fists so much,
That he became one.
A threat,
Something to dunk and dive,
Away from,
A screaming ball of muscles and anger.
My dad.
The fist.
Same thing, right?
There's another you that I remember!
This one is etched into my brain,

It's the one I run from daily,
The one I can't quite escape,
The man with the changing face.
The eyes,
That scan my body,
As if it is a prize,
You can claim!
Your hands forever reaching,
Searching,
Wandering,
My body,
As part of your little game.
I remember your clothes,
The way you walked,
Stomping your feet.
Your pants that always fell,
And my body being crushed,
Under your weight.
I remember you,
As yellowing teeth,
Never brushed,
Laughing in my face.
I remember you in the most revolting,
Kind of ways!
I remember you as my first heartbreak,
The one that taught me,
How not to behave!
The one that taught me,
How I don't want to be treated!
I remember you as a fist,
The fist that never changed.
It used me and abused me,
And turned my body,
Black and blue,
Then yellow and green.
It silenced my screams,
It stopped the tears,
It reached inside,

Gripped the beating heart,
And tore it out of my chest.
Leaving me with the broken pieces,
The dark memories,
Just parting gifts,
To remind me of your lessons.
You were never my father!
You were the fist,
That turned me into a crime scene!
My body is just evidence,
Of how you behaved.

Crime scenes

I am a crime scene.
The one you left in your wake.
Dressed in caution tape,
Invisible to the human eye,
But still, nobody dares approach me,
They treat me like a fragile,
Easily broken object.
So beaten and worn,
It couldn't take the slightest touch!
And so their arms never embrace me,
Their hands never hold mine,
Their words dance around,
The memory of you,
As though just the thought of you,
Would make me collapse.
But I am not made of glass!
I have been beaten,
And torn,
And shattered,
And then I put myself back together,
Painted this smile back on my face!
Because you changed me,
Sure.
But I refuse to let you break me,
Or end me in any way!
I used to be a crime scene,
But I washed the memory of you away.
Your fingerprints no longer mark me,
The blood has been scrubbed away,
The bruises have disappeared,
And time has replaced each cell in my body.
Each part of me you touched,
Is no longer tainted!
And I am slicing,

And peeling away,
At the yellow tape.
Aren't you proud of me?
I can clean up crime scenes too!
I can destroy evidence!
I can create a new life for myself!
I can forget your existence!
I learnt from the best,
Aren't you proud of me?

I Was a Kid

You told me I deserved it,
I thought that it was true,
Ignored all the people in my life,
That told me I didn't,
I believed you.
Now I realise,
That was the lie you told yourself,
That I deserved what you did,
That I made you angry,
I was a bad child,
Did it help to blame your actions on me?
I don't believe you anymore,
Your point of view was twisted,
Your words not to be trusted,
The people that support me would never do what you did.
So it's them I believe now,
Despite what you said,
I never deserved what you did,
I was a fucking kid!!!

A Five-Year-Old's Story

At five years old,
All I could do was survive.
A child forged from a loveless marriage,
I'd seen things children,
Shouldn't be able to describe!
At sixteen years old,
I spoke up for the child,
Who kept secrets,
No child should ever hold.
Asked them to help me,
In my search for justice,
For a child,
Who was never told:
That there are some places,
Hands shouldn't wander,
When you're only five years old!
And when that burden got too much,
I found myself needing help,
In a rather scary ward,
Where I slowly lost myself.
At eighteen years old,
I felt unsafe,
Everywhere I went!
Because a judge decided,
Eighteen is an age,
Where you can defend yourself.
But I thought the only way to do that,
Was to leave this world behind,
If I wasn't here,
He couldn't hurt me,
Like he did as a child.
At nineteen years old,
My body protested,
It seized,

It froze itself,
And I began to wonder,
What I'd done to deserve,
This fluctuating hell.
At twenty years old,
I was homeless,
With nowhere safe to go,
Attempting to live my own life,
I left my past behind.
At twenty-one years old,
I can tell my story,
Not flinch away at all.
Because that five-year-old,
Was let down by adults,
I refuse to do the same!
When people tell me their troubles,
I embrace my old pain.
At that moment I know,
A five-year-old's story,
Holds more power,
Than I knew,
Because when I tell it now,
People find the strength,
To whisper "Me Too".